Doctors

Then and Now

Sarah Kartchner Clark, M.A.

Contributing Author
Jill K. Mulhall, M.Ed.

Associate Editor
Christina Hill, M.A.

Assistant Editor
Torrey Maloof

Editorial Director
Emily R. Smith, M.A.Ed.

Project Researcher
Gillian Eve Makepeace

Editor-in-Chief
Sharon Coan, M.S.Ed.

Editorial Manager
Gisela Lee, M.A.

Creative Director
Lee Aucoin

Illustration Manager
Timothy J. Bradley

Designers
Debora Brown
Lesley Palmer
Zac Calbert
Robin Erickson

Project Consultant
Corinne Burton, M.A.Ed.

Publisher
Rachelle Cracchiolo, M.S.Ed.

Teacher Created Materials

5301 Oceanus Drive
Huntington Beach, CA 92649
http://www.tcmpub.com
ISBN 978-0-7439-9373-9
© *2007 Teacher Created Materials, Inc.*

Table of Contents

What Is a Doctor?

Doctors are an important part of our community (kuh-MEW-nuh-TEE). They help us stay healthy. They teach us how to take care of our bodies. And, they help us get well when we are sick.

There are many things doctors can do to help their **patients** (PAY-shuntz). Doctors can listen to people's bodies with special tools. And, doctors can give people **medicine** (MED-uh-sin) when they need it.

A tool used to listen ➡ to heartbeats

A doctor ➡ gives a patient a shot.

A doctor ➡ talks to her young patient.

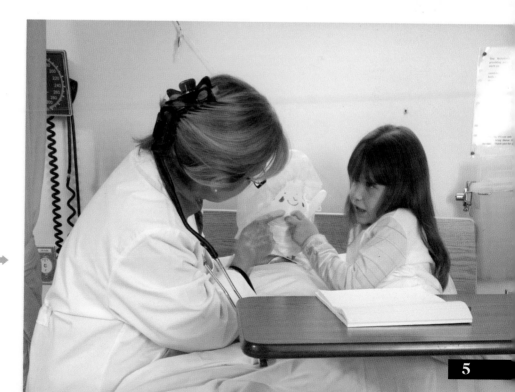

How to Become a Doctor

What do you want to be when you grow up? If you want to be a doctor, it takes a lot of hard work. Doctors have to go to school for a long time. They go for at least seven years of school after high school. There is a special school for people who want to be doctors. It is called **medical** (MED-uh-kuhl) school.

You need good grades to go to medical school. Medical students take many science classes. They learn about how our bodies work. They learn how to tell what kind of sickness a person has. After a lot of studying and practice, they become doctors.

Schools in Other Lands

There are medical schools all around the world. These schools may teach different things. So, any doctor who wants to work in the United States must pass a special test. That way, they can prove they have all the skills needed to be good doctors.

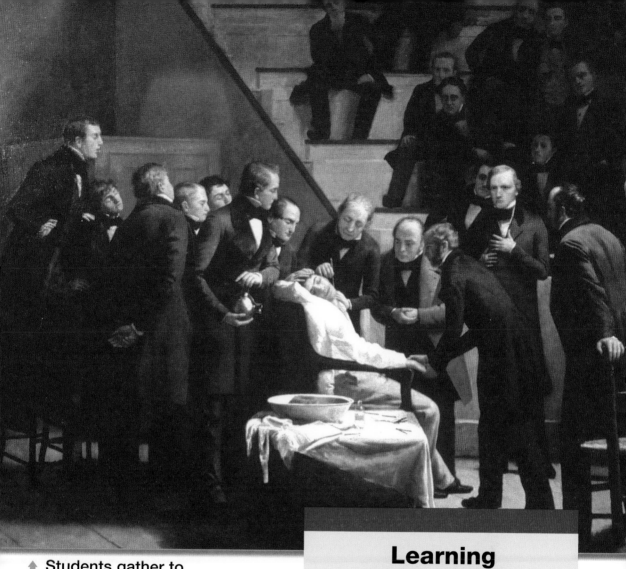

▲ Students gather to
watch a doctor work.

◀ A medical student uses a
microscope (MY-kruh-skohp).

Learning
from Others

Long ago, there were no medical
schools. But, there were people
who wanted to be doctors. They
would follow the doctors from
town to town. And, they would
watch the doctors work. This is
how they learned.

A Doctor's Tools

There are a lot of tools that doctors use. These tools help them know what is going on inside their patients' bodies.

Each tool is used to check different things. A **stethoscope** (STETH-uh-skope) lets the doctor hear how fast your heart is beating. An **otoscope** (oh-tuh-SKOPE) is used to look inside your ears. A **thermometer** (thur-MOM-uh-tuhr) tells the doctor your body **temperature** (TEMP-uhr-uh-chuhr).

A doctor's bag ➡ holds many tools.

A doctor ➡ taps your knee with a reflex hammer.

Tools of the Time

Doctor's tools have changed through the years. Doctors used to carry all of their tools in one black bag. The tools were very simple. Now, tools are complex. Many of the new tools are expensive. Sometimes doctors share them.

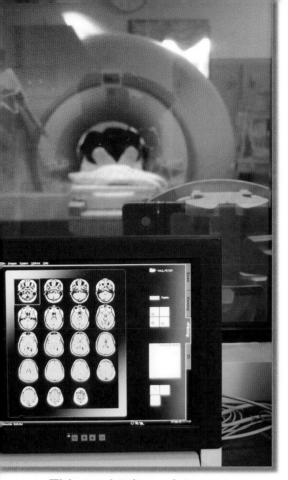

▲ This tool takes pictures of the brain.

▲ A doctor uses a stethoscope to listen to the girl's heartbeat.

Today, doctors use a tool called an **X-ray machine**. They use it to take pictures of our bones.

Miracle Medicines

Long ago, doctors did not have medicines like today. They used dried plants to help sick people. These did not always work. So, scientists worked hard. They created new medicines. Now, doctors can use medicine in lots of ways. Some medicines can make a sickness go away. Others help people to not get sick.

Where Do Doctors Work?

Doctors work in many places. Some doctors work in hospitals. This is where sick people go to get better. Doctors take care of the sick people. They check on them every day. This is how they make sure their patients are doing better.

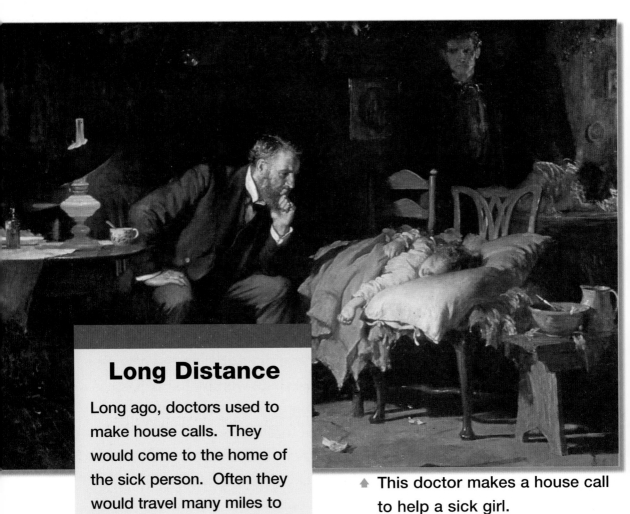

Long Distance

Long ago, doctors used to make house calls. They would come to the home of the sick person. Often they would travel many miles to get there.

⬆ This doctor makes a house call to help a sick girl.

Doctors Around the World

There are many communities around the world. Some do not have enough doctors. Doctors from around the world will travel to these places. They try to help. They do not always have the tools and medicines that they need. But, these doctors do the best they can. They help a lot of sick people.

▲ Some doctors travel to Africa.

Some doctors work in medical offices. This is where people come to see the doctor for a visit. Other doctors work in nursing homes. Some older people live in nursing homes. They need a lot of care by doctors.

Types of Doctors

There are many types of doctors. Some doctors treat one part of the body. There are doctors for your eyes. There are doctors for your ears, nose and throat. There are even doctors just for your feet!

Other doctors learn to treat the whole body. They work in offices called family practices. They see patients of all ages. But, there are other doctors just for children. They are called **pediatricians** (pee-dee-uh-TRIH-shuhns). And, there are doctors that help women have babies.

Getting the Medicine

People get sick. They need medicine. It helps them get well. Doctors know what kind of medicine is needed. The name of that medicine is given to a **pharmacist** (FAR-muh-sist). Pharmacists measure the medicine and make sure it is safe. And, they answer questions.

A drugstore in ➡ Washington, D.C.

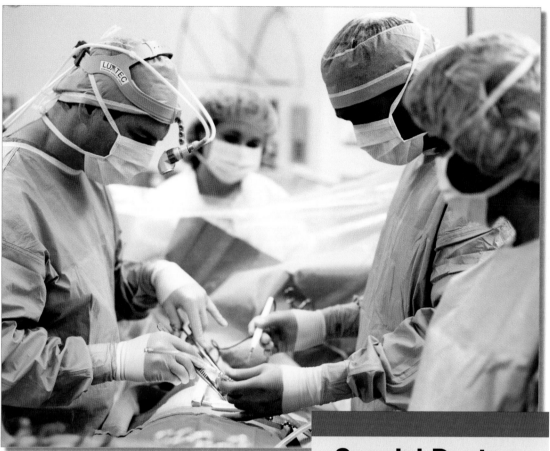

⬆ Surgeons operate on a patient

Special Doctors

Some doctors are called **surgeons** (SUHR-juhnz). Their jobs are very hard. They **operate** on people. That means that they fix things inside people's bodies. This can help save people's lives.

⬆ A pediatrician

What Makes a Good Doctor?

▲ This doctor lets his patient use his stethoscope.

What does it take to be a good doctor? Doctors need to be hard workers. They work very long hours. Sometimes they work whole days without stopping.

A doctor can be a man or a woman. Doctors spend a lot of time with people. So, they need to be kind and caring. This is called having a good **bedside manner**. Doctors also need to be able to make big decisions (dih-SIZ-uhns). And, they need to make these decisions quickly.

Important Promises

All doctors have to take an **oath**. It is called the Hippocratic Oath (hih-puh-KRA-tik ohth). It is named after a doctor. He lived in 400 B.C. The doctors promise not to hurt anyone on purpose. They promise to be kind to their patients. And, they promise to do what they can to help people.

Elizabeth Blackwell

Ms. Doctor

Elizabeth Blackwell wanted to be a doctor. At that time, there were no female doctors. People laughed at her for wanting to be a doctor. It took her a long time to get into medical school. But, finally she did. She was the first woman to become a doctor.

⬇ X-rays help doctors treat patients.

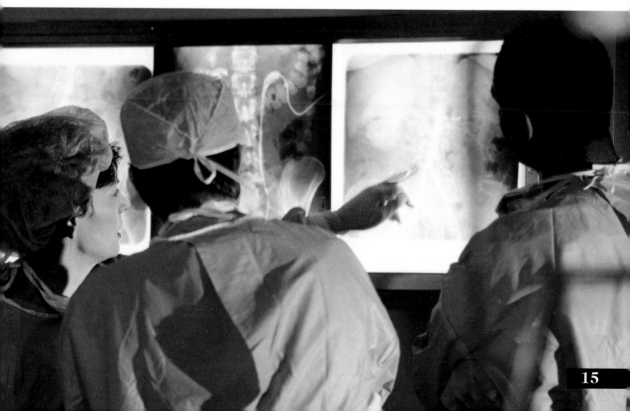

A Doctor Needs Help

There are lots of people who help doctors. Nurses work with doctors to help treat patients. A nurse weighs you on the scale. A nurse will also take your blood pressure and your temperature. This saves time for the doctor.

▲ Many people work together to help patients.

Office workers fill out papers and write on charts. They also answer phones. It takes a lot of people to help doctors take care of patients.

Helpers for No Pay

Volunteers (VOL-uhn-teerz) are people who like to help others. They do not get paid to work. They help in hospitals. Doctors need their help. Some volunteers were once called "candy stripers." This is because they wore red-and-white striped uniforms.

Florence Nightingale

Florence Nightingale

Nurses help doctors. They have done so for many years. One famous nurse was Florence Nightingale (FLOR-uhnz NI-tuhn-gale). In 1851, she was in charge of a hospital in London. It was very dirty. She knew that hospitals need to be clean and in order. So, she cleaned it up. This changed the way hospitals were kept.

What Are Diseases?

As long as people have lived, there have been **diseases** (dih-ZEEZ-uhz). Diseases make people sick. Some people get better. But, some do not.

Long ago, millions of people died from an awful disease. It was called The Black Death. Another disease called small pox made lots of people sick, too.

⬇ A child receives a shot.

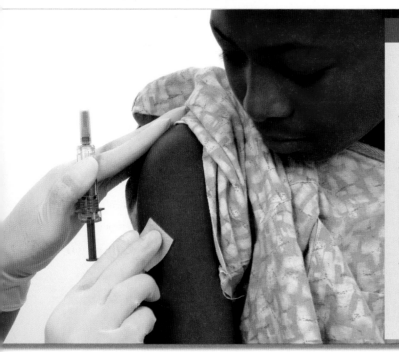

Shots That Save People

Vaccines (vak-SEENS) are medicines. They keep us from getting sick. They are given in shots. Vaccines can save us from getting diseases. Most people start to get vaccines when they are babies. Have you ever had a vaccine shot?

Doctors did not know what made people sick. Then, they learned about germs. They learned that people could keep from getting sick if they kept clean.

A sick man ➡ receives medicine.

Alexander Fleming

Germ Killers

In 1942, Alexander Fleming discovered a mold that would kill **bacteria** (bak-TIHR-ee-uh). He found this mold growing on his dirty dishes. Gross! The mold was made into a medicine. It is called **penicillin** (peh-nuh-SIH-luhn). It fights germs in our bodies. This medicine has saved many lives.

Times Have Changed

Things have changed through the years for doctors. Today, they can do amazing things to help people.

There have been a lot of new inventions. A pacemaker is a new invention. It helps a heart beat smoothly. Doctors can now replace sick body parts with healthy new ones. And, they can use X-rays to see inside bodies.

🔻 This doctor studies pictures of the brain.

Looking to the Future

What will happen in the future? Maybe there will be new medicines. Or, there may be new types of **surgeries**. New machines (muh-SHEENZ) may make it easier to see inside the body.

Doctors now know how people can stay healthy. They tell us to get plenty of exercise. They know which foods we should eat. They remind us to wear sunblock.

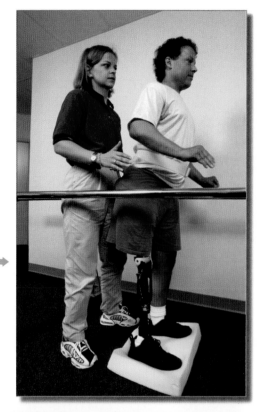

This man is starting to exercise ➡ again after losing his leg.

A Change of Heart

In 1628, William Harvey wrote a report. He said that the heart was actually a pump. He explained that the heart worked like a water pump. This shocked a lot of people. Later, in 1967, the first **heart transplant** was done.

This drawing shows ➡ how the heart and lungs work together.

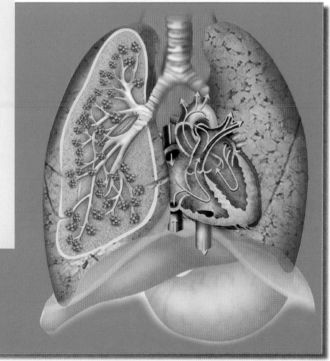

Call the Doctor

Doctors can help us get well and stay healthy. Doctors teach us healthy habits. Your doctor will tell you to eat healthy food. And, get lots of sleep and exercise. These are things that will help you to not get sick.

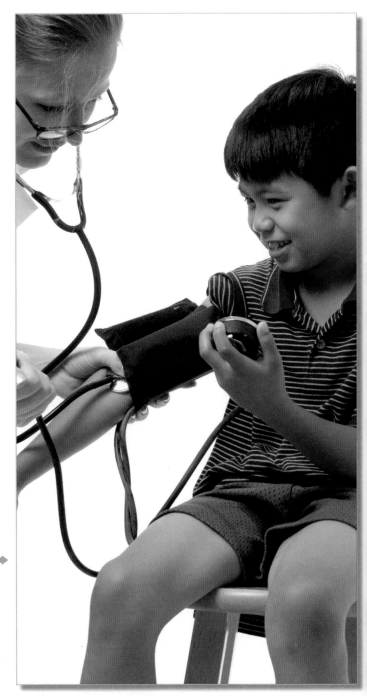

A doctor checks ➡ a child's blood pressure.

Doctors are always learning. There are new inventions and a lot of new information to learn every day. Doctors can cure sicknesses. And, they can save lives. Being a doctor is a hard job. But, it is a very important one.

Doctors operate on a patient.

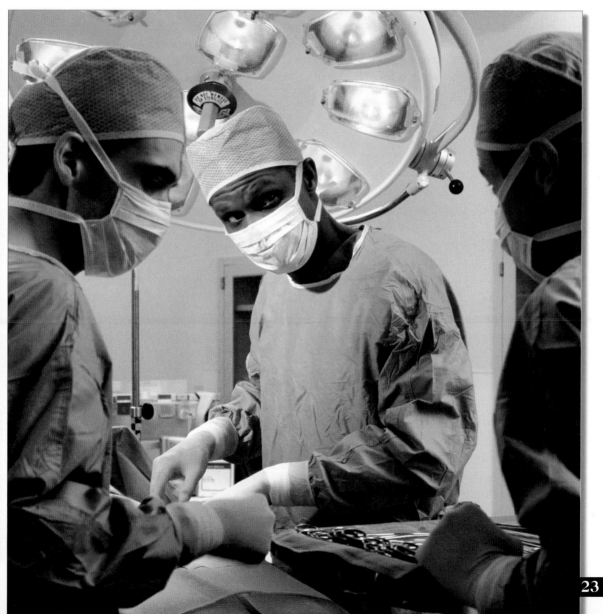

A Day in the Life Then

Elizabeth Blackwell (1821–1910)

Elizabeth Blackwell wanted to be a doctor. But, women could not go to medical school. She was turned away from every school but one. She went to medical school in New York. The people there did not want her to come. But, that did not stop her. Soon the people of New York did not mind that she was a woman. She was a good doctor.

Let's pretend to ask Elizabeth Blackwell some questions about her job.

Why did you decide to be a doctor?

I wanted to do something new. I thought medicine was interesting. I think women can do any job. They just need the chance.

What is your day like?

I travel a lot. I talk to students who are at school. When I am home, I work as a doctor. I help women and children.

↟ Blackwell worked with the United States Sanitary Commission (sa-nuh-TEHR-ee kuh-MIH-shuhn). This group trained nurses.

What do you like most about your job?

I get to heal people. I am happy when I help people feel better. Now that I am a doctor, more women are going to medical school. Soon, more women will be doctors. That is important to me.

Tools of the Trade Then

Doctors began using **syringes** (suh-RINJ-es) ➤
in the late 1800s. They were useful tools.
Doctors could give medicine with syringes.
This kept people healthy.

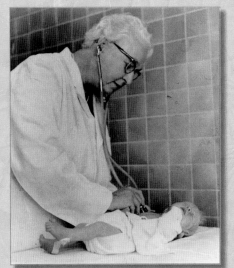

◀ This doctor used a stethoscope. This
tool helped her listen to the baby's
heartbeat. You have probably had
a doctor listen to your heart with a
stethoscope. They are still used today.

Doctors used to make many ➤
house calls. They would bring a
kit like this. It held their tools.

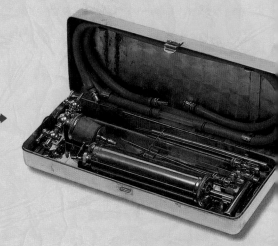

◀ Doctors used to wear this on their
heads. The mirror would help shine
light. It made it easier for doctors to
see. Now, doctors have special lights
to help them see.

Tools of the Trade Now

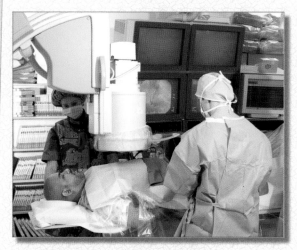

This is a new syringe. Doctors use them only once. Then, they throw them away. That way, germs do not spread.

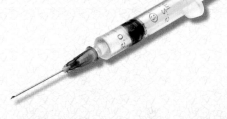

▲ This is an X-ray machine. It helps doctors see inside our bodies.

This doctor is doing a CAT scan ▶ of a patient. This machine takes pictures of the brain.

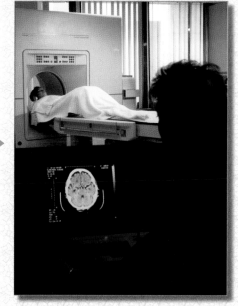

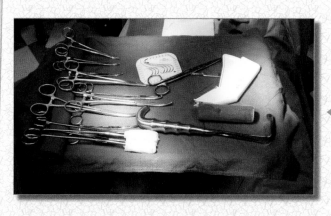

◀ Surgeons use tools like this. They are used to help fix problems on the inside of patients' bodies.

A Day in the Life Now

Kinnari Desai

Kinnari Desai (kih-NAR-ee DEH-si) is a special doctor. She is a pediatrician. That means that she only works with babies and children. She helps them feel better when they are sick. When Dr. Desai was young, she was often sick. She needed to see the doctor a lot. Now, she is a doctor. She helps children in her community.

Why did you decide to become a doctor?

I think I've always wanted to become a doctor. Doctors get a lot of respect. And it feels great to help patients. I decided to become a pediatrician during my last year of medical school. I like to help children.

What is your day like?

I enjoy the different things I face each day. Some are fun and exciting. Others are more difficult. But, the great thing about being a doctor is that no day is the same. I work in lots of areas and do different things. I see lots of patients. This makes my day unique.

What do you like most about your job?

The best part of my job is when I can figure out a problem. Then, I can offer solutions to children who are ill. I like to ease the fears

of parents. I work hard to cure children's illnesses. I know this will bring their parents joy.

◄ Dr. Desai works in a big hospital.

Glossary

bacteria—tiny living things that can make people sick

bedside manner—kind and caring treatment shown by doctors

diseases—illnesses or sicknesses

heart transplant—to put a new heart into someone's body

medical—having to do with doctors or medicine

medicine—pills or syrup used to treat a sickness

microscope—a tool that makes things look bigger in size

oath—a promise you make very seriously

operate—to work on the inside of someone's body

otoscope—a tool that checks inside your ears, nose, and throat

patients—people who go to visit the doctor

pediatricians—doctors who take care of children

penicillin—a medicine that kills bacteria

pharmacist—a person who is trained to give out medicine

stethoscope—a special instrument used to listen to a heartbeat

surgeons—doctors who do operations

surgeries—the work done on the inside of someone's body by a doctor

syringes—tools that put medicine into the body

temperature—degree of hot or cold

thermometer—an instrument used to check body temperature

vaccines—shots that help protect people from diseases

volunteers—people who help others for free

X-ray machine—a special machine that takes photos of the bones inside the body

Index

Credits

Acknowledgements

Special thanks to Kinnari Desai for providing the *Day in the Life Now* interview. Dr. Desai is a doctor in Loma Linda, California.

Image Credits

cover Comstock Images; p.1 Comstock Images; p.4 (left) Hemera Technologies, Inc.; p.4 (right) Comstock Images; p.5 (top) Colorado Historical Society; p.5 (bottom) Photos.com; p.6 Comstock Images; p.7 The Granger Collection, New York; p.8 (top) Photos.com; p. 8 (bottom) Photos.com; p.9 (left) Photos.com; p.9 (right) Photos.com; p.10 The Granger Collection, New York; p.11 Daniel Pepper/Getty Images; p.12 The Library of Congress; p.13 (top) Photos.com; p.13 (bottom) Photos.com; p.14 Photos.com; p.15 (top) The Granger Collection, New York; p.15 (bottom) Comstock Images; p.16 Comstock Images; p.17 The Library of Congress; p.18 iStockphoto.com/Jaimie Duplass; p.19 (top) The Granger Collection, New York; p.19 (bottom) The Granger Collection, New York; p.20 Comstock Images; p.21 (top) Brand X Pictures; p.21 (bottom) Nick Neese; p.22 GeoM/Shutterstock, Inc.; p.23 Comstock Images; p.24 The Granger Collection, New York; p.25 The Library of Congress; p.26 (top) Clipart.com; p.26 (middle left) The Library of Congress; p.26 (middle right) Clipart.com; p.26 (bottom) Clipart.com; p.27 (top left) Photos.com; p.27 (top right) Andrea Leone/Shutterstock, Inc.; p.27 (center) Photos.com; p.27 (bottom) iStockphoto.com/Susan Campbell; p.28 Courtesy of Kinnari Desai; p.29 Galina Barskaya/Shutterstock, Inc.; back cover Denver Public Library